Saying goodbye to...
A Friend

Dorset Libraries
Withdrawn Stock

Dorset County Library		
204298279 ○		
Askews	2005	
	£5.99	

DORSET COUNTY LIBRARY

204298279 0

Chrysalis

First published in the UK in 2003 by
Chrysalis Children's Books
An imprint of Chrysalis Books Group Plc
The Chrysalis Building
Bramley Road
London W10 6SP

Paperback edition first published in 2005

Text © Chrysalis Books Group Plc 2003
Illustrations © Chrysalis Books Group Plc 2003

Text by Nicola Edwards

Editorial manager: Joyce Bentley
Senior editor: Sarah Nunn
Project editor: Jean Coppendale
Designer: Clare Sleven
Illustrations by: Sarah Roper
Picture researcher: Jenny Barlow
Consultant: Jenni Thomas, Chief Executive The
Child Bereavement Trust

All rights reserved. No part of this book may be
reproduced or utilized in any form or by any
means, electronic or mechanical,
including photocopying, recording or by any
information storage and retrieval
system,without written permission from
the publisher, except by a reviewer who may
quote passages in a review.

ISBN 1 84138 836 X (hb)
ISBN 1 84458 466 6 (pb)

British Library Cataloguing in Publication Data
for this book is available from the British
Library.

Printed in China

All reasonable efforts have been made to trace the relevant copyright holders of the images contained within
this book. If we were unable to reach you, please contact Chrysalis Children's Books.

Cover Getty Images/Terry Vine 1 Format/Mo Wilson 4 Bubbles/Angela Hampton 5 Bubbles/David Robinson 6
Getty Images/Eyewire Collection 7 Corbis/O'Brien Productions 8 Rex/Alex Woods (PNS) 9 Format/Mo Wilson
10 Getty Images/Photodisc/Mel Curtis 11 Corbis/Reza/Webistan 12 Getty Images/Catherine Ledner 13
Corbis/Laura Dwight 14 Bubbles/Jennie Woodcock 15 John Birdsall 16 Bubbles/Fiona Adams 17
Bubbles/David Robinson 18 Corbis/Little Blue Wolf Productions 19 Getty Images/Mary Kate Denny 20
Corbis/Royalty Free/Image 100 21 Getty Images/Photodisc/SW Productions 22 Corbis/Tim Thompson 23
Corbis/David Bartruff 24 Getty Images/Photodisc/Ryan McVay 25 Impact Photos/Christopher Cormack 26
Getty Images/Jim Cummins 27 and 28 Bubbles/Angela Hampton 29 Bubbles/David Robinson.

Foreword

Confronting death and dying as an adult is
difficult but addressing these issues with
children is even harder. Children need to
hear the truth and sharing a book can
encourage and help both adults and
children to talk openly and honestly about
their feelings, something many of us find
difficult to do.

Written in a clear, sensitive and very caring
way, the **Saying Goodbye To...** series will
help parents, carers and teachers to meet the
needs of grieving children. Reading about
the variety of real life situations, including
the death of a pet, may enable children to
feel less alone and more able to make sense
of the bewildering emotions and responses
they feel when someone dies.

Being alongside grieving children is not
easy, the **Saying Goodbye To...** series will
help make this challenging task a little less
daunting.

Jenni Thomas OBE
Chief Executive
The Child Bereavement Trust

The Child Bereavement Trust
Registered Charity No. 04049

Contents

Dorset Libraries
Withdrawn Stock

So unfair

Children's friends are an important part of their lives. They enjoy being with friends they like and **trust**. So when a child's friend dies it's very sad and difficult for them to **accept**.

Friends can make each other happy.

Their friend might have been a child, too. When a friend dies it can seem very wrong and unfair that such a young life has ended so soon.

Gaby and Tami are best friends. They never stop talking!

Something to think about...
When a friend dies it's hard to make sense of what has happened. It can help to talk to someone you know who will understand how you are feeling.

Illness and dying

Sometimes children die because of an illness, such as cancer. They may be unwell for a long time before they die. Some children can still go to school, even if they are very sick. Others may have to stay at home or in hospital or **hospice**. Their friends can visit them, phone them and send them letters and videos.

Laura looked forward to visits from her friend, Josie.

Something to think about...
Children who are ill often say they like their friends
to behave normally around them. They don't want to
be treated differently because they are ill.

Charley wanted to go to school even though she was ill. She liked being
with her friends.

A terrible shock

Sometimes children die suddenly, for example, in an accident at home or on holiday. Some children are killed in road accidents.

When a child dies suddenly it's very hard for anyone to make sense of what has happened.

Children have also been killed deliberately, although this does not happen very often. When a child dies suddenly it's a terrible shock. It's frightening and very upsetting.

Children often help and support each other when a friend dies.

Something to think about...

When a friend dies it's natural to worry that the same thing will happen to you. But most children grow up safely without being involved in serious accidents.

Angry and confused

Children often go through many different feelings when a friend dies. They may feel angry with life for being cruel and unfair. It may seem to them that the world isn't a safe place any more. They may want to **blame** adults for not being able to stop their friend dying. They may even be cross with their friend for dying and leaving them to feel sad.

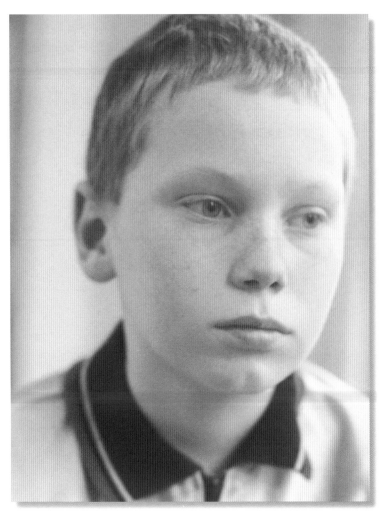

At first, Tom was angry with his mum when his friend, Joe, died. He didn't think she understood how he was feeling.

When Naeem was killed in a car accident, his friends felt angry with the drivers of cars.

Something to think about...
It's normal to feel that the world has been turned upside-down when a friend dies. It can help to talk about your feelings with someone you trust.

Feeling guilty

Children can feel **guilty** when a friend dies. They may feel bad about the times when they were **jealous** of their friend, or when they were unkind or mean to them.

Mehmet was upset when his friend, Mark, died. They'd had an argument and hadn't had a chance to make up.

Some children may feel guilty because they couldn't do anything to stop their friend dying. They may wish they'd had a chance to say goodbye.

Sean wrote a letter to his friend, George, to say sorry for the times when he'd said unkind things to her.

Something to think about...
It's natural to feel guilty, and to think your friend may have died because of something you said or did. But children are not to blame for the death of a friend.

13

Feeling scared

Thinking about death and dying can be scary. When a friend dies, it may be the first time a child has thought about death. If their friend died after being ill, children may worry about becoming ill themselves.

It helped Euan to talk to his dad when his friend, Peter, died.

Something to think about...
Writing down what you are feeling or drawing a picture can sometimes help you to show how you feel.

If a child's friend dies in a terrible accident, they may be very worried that the same thing will happen to them. They may be scared that they will be the next to die.

When Lucy died, her friends had the chance to talk to their teacher about her death and share their happy memories of her.

15

Asking questions

When a friend dies, children need help to understand what has happened. Adults sometimes try to **protect** children from painful feelings by not talking openly and clearly about the death. But this only makes children more confused and upset. Children often need to ask the same questions over and over again.

When Hettie died, her friends found it helpful to talk to each other.

Jane's mum cuddled her and helped her when her friend, Anthony, died.

Something to think about...
It's normal to have lots of questions when
a friend dies. Adults can help, even though they may not
have all the answers.

Feeling sad and lonely

When a friend dies it's natural to feel very upset and to miss them a lot. Children whose friend has died may feel like crying. This can be a good way of letting out feelings of sadness.

When Josh died, his friend Sanjay felt sad when he saw Josh's empty chair at school. It reminded Sanjay how much he was going to miss Josh.

Something to think about...
When you feel sad about your friend, it's good to think of the happy times that you spent together and what you'll remember about them.

But not everyone feels like crying. This doesn't mean they're not feeling sad.

*Natalie's teacher **comforted** her when she felt sad because her best friend Anna had died.*

19

Being a friend

The death of a child is a shocking thing to happen to a family. When a friend dies, children often wish they could do something to help their friend's family.

Sophie drew a special picture of her friend, Leah. She sent it to Leah's mum and dad.

Some children send a letter or a card to their friend's parents. It can be comforting for parents to know how much their child meant to their friends.

Photos reminded Maxine of the happy holidays she spent with her friend, Paula, and Paula's family.

Something to think about...
If you want to, you could write to your friend's parents to tell them what a good friend their child was to you.

21

A chance to say goodbye

Sometimes children are invited to go to the **funeral** of a friend. A funeral is a special service which gives people who cared about a person who has died the chance to remember them and say goodbye. There are different types of funeral. Some are **religious** and others are not, because different people have different beliefs. People often feel sad at a funeral, but everyone is there to **comfort** each other.

At this funeral procession, people comfort each other as they walk behind the coffin and show their respect for the person who has died.

Something to think about...
It's natural to feel worried about going to a funeral.
But people will be there to help you.

Sometimes children take part in funerals by lighting candles, reading poems or choosing songs for everyone to sing.

23

Remembering a friend

It helps children to **grieve** if they can keep hold of their memories of the friend who has died. Making a collection of photos can help. So can writing down or drawing memories of the friend – such as what they said and did, the things they liked and disliked, their favourite music and television programmes.

Mia and Jo remembered how much their friend, Katy, liked singing when they watched videos of the concerts they'd been in together at school.

Saying goodbye to a friend

When Nathan
died, his friends
at school raised
money for charity
in memory of him.

Something to do...
You could make a list of the things that made your
friend special and the things that you'd like to
remember about them.

25

Difficult days

When a child's friend dies it's normal for them not to feel sad all the time. But they may find that they suddenly miss their friend when they're in the middle of a game, or watching television.

During James's birthday outing he thought about his friend, Robbie, and wished he could have been there to share the fun.

They can also miss their friend on special days such as their birthday. It makes them sad to think that they would have spent the day together.

The children in Pretti's class planted a tree in memory of her.

Feeling happy again

When a friend dies, it's natural to feel shocked and upset. Grieving is natural and everyone grieves in their own way – there are no rules to follow. After a while, it's normal for different memories to replace the sad and painful feelings which were so difficult when the person first died.

Jonathan was proud that he'd been David's best friend.

After a friend has died, children can feel guilty when they realize they're having fun and not thinking about their friend as much. But feeling happy again is a natural part of grieving.

William's friends would never forget him.

Glossary

accept	to believe that something is true
blame	to think that something bad is someone's fault
comfort	to help someone who is sad to feel better
funeral	a special service in which people remember a person who has died and say goodbye to them
grieve	to feel very sad after someone has died
guilty	feeling bad, as if it's your fault that something is wrong
hospice	a building where people who are dying are looked after
jealous	wishing that what someone else has could be yours
protect	to take care of someone and keep them from harm
reassure	to comfort someone and take away their worries
religious	to do with a belief in God
trust	to feel that someone will not let you down

Useful addresses

The Child Bereavement Trust

A charity offering training, resources and support for professional carers and teachers working with bereaved children and grieving adults
Aston House
High Street
West Wycombe
Bucks HP14 3AG
Tel: 01494 446648
Information and Support Line: 0845 357 1000
E-mail: enquiries@childbereavement.org.uk
Website: www.childbereavement.org.uk
* New interactive website where children and adults can send emails

Childhood Bereavement Network

An organization offering bereaved children and their families and caregivers information about the support services available to them.
Huntingdon House
278-290 Huntingdon Street
Nottingham NG1 3LY
Tel: 0115 911 8070
E-mail: cbn@ncb.org.uk
Website: www.ncb.org.uk/cbn

ChildLine

Childline's free, 24-hour helpline is staffed by trained counsellors, offering help and support to children and young people. The website includes information on bereavement.
Freepost 1111
London N1 0BR
Tel: 0800 11 11 (Freephone 24 hours)
Website: www.childline.org.uk

Cruse Bereavement Care

The Cruse helpline offers information and counselling to people of all ages who have been bereaved. The website offers additional information and support.

Cruse House
126 Sheen Road
Richmond
Surrey TW9 1UR
Tel: 020 8322 7227
Helpline: 0870 167 1677 (Mondays to Fridays 9.30am-5pm)
Website: www.crusebereavementcare.org.uk

The Samaritans

An organization offering support and help to anyone who is emotionally distressed.
Tel: 08457 90 90 90 (24 hours)
Website: www.samaritans.org.uk

Winston's Wish

A charity offering support and information to bereaved children and their families.
The Clara Burgess Centre
Gloucestershire Royal Hospital
Great Western Road
Gloucester GL1 3NN
Tel: 01452 394377
Family Line: 0845 20 30 40 5 (Mondays to Fridays 9.30am-5pm)
E-mail: info@winstonswish.org.uk
Website: www.winstonswish.org

Youth Access

An organization providing information about youth counselling services.
1-2 Taylors Yard
67 Alderbrook Road
London SW12 8AD
Tel: 020 8772 9900 (Monday to Fridays 9am-1pm, 2-5pm)
E-mail: admin@youthaccess.org.uk

Index